TULA

TULA

POEMS

CHRIS SANTIAGO

MILKWEED EDITIONS

Published 2016 by Milkweed Editions
Printed in Canada
Cover design and art by Mary Austin Speaker
Frontispiece art by Yuri Santiago
Author photo by Joanna Demkiewicz
16 17 18 19 20 5 4 3 2 1
First Edition

Milkweed Editions, an independent nonprofit publisher, gratefully acknowledges sustaining support from the Jerome Foundation; the Lindquist & Vennum Foundation; the McKnight Foundation; the National Endowment for the Arts; the Target Foundation; and other generous contributions from foundations, corporations, and individuals. Also, this activity is made possible by the voters of Minnesota through a Minnesota State Arts Board Operating Support grant, thanks to a legislative appropriation from the arts and cultural heritage fund, and a grant from the Wells Fargo Foundation Minnesota. For a full listing of Milkweed Editions supporters, please visit www.milkweed.org.

Library of Congress Cataloging-in-Publication Data

Names: Santiago, Chris, author.
Title: Tula : poems / Chris Santiago.
Description: First edition. | Minneapolis, Minnesota : Milkweed Editions, 2016.
Identifiers: LCCN 2016030738 (print) | LCCN 2016038345 (ebook) | ISBN 9781571314888 (paperback) | ISBN 9781571319548 (e-book)
Subjects: | BISAC: POETRY / American / General.
Classification: LCC PS3619.A573 A6 2016 (print) | LCC PS3619.A573 (ebook) | DDC 811/.6--dc23
LC record available at https://lccn.loc.gov/2016030738

Milkweed Editions is committed to ecological stewardship. We strive to align our book production practices with this principle, and to reduce the impact of our operations in the environment. We are a member of the Green Press Initiative, a nonprofit coalition of publishers, manufacturers, and authors working to protect the world's endangered forests and conserve natural resources. *Tula* was printed on acid-free 100% postconsumer-waste paper by Friesens Corporation.

For Yuri
for our mothers & fathers
for their mothers & fathers
& for our sons

Contents

tu · la |'toōlə|

Nahuatl: near the cattails; ruined Toltec capital. Tall
atlantes, sun-cut shields. God-nest. Birdsong. Mongolian:
willow-banked tributary of the Orkhon. Baltic: unreach-
able, Russified to oblast. Ironworks. Hollow points. Music
box gilt & nielloed with orchids, islands, passerines;
tula-work. Chileno: slang for cock. Also nightshade, bell-
flower. Solfege: veil & a sixth. English: square-rigged for
new continents. Almost marsh grass, ghosted to Caddo.
Kotule: savanna tongue, rich in affix, in use by all genera-
tions. Sanskrit: Libra. Scales, stars above our son. *Was* the
weight of *will.* Nahuatl from the Nahuatl for 'what pleases
the ear.' Tagalog: an aporia. Mother tongue: a poem.

Audiometry

Because my son thinks I am a citadel—
soundproof. A repository.

Because horsing around at bedtime he pierced
my cochlea with a pencil.

The first time I saw the inner ear
I thought it looked like a little life, thriving

but not yet big enough
for me to feel for it any kind of empathy.

By what were such things fed?
Would it overgrow its carapace

& make of the body a coppered bell?
And then I was sixteen & crossing

Saint Paul with my father. A seashell
in his pocket which for his own reasons

he refuses to wear. He can't hear
the Chicano keeping pace behind us,

lean & loose-limbed,
clucking, "Gooks, gooks."

For years, he'd sat a little further from us
each night at the dinner table

hollowed out by the roll of stock tickers
all through his graveyard hours.

It's a remarkable machine
the nurse slides into my ear canal, built

to detect lies & arrhythmia & the trembling
of incalculable tranches of earth.

I pulled his pace toward mine but declined
to parse his solitude for him—planes

of salt-haloed stone refusing
to let footfalls cut to their holdings.

Tula

The linnet will be singing.
A man will awaken on his deathbed,
not yet cured.

—LARRY LEVIS

Blood stranger,
we never met: you died so far away
that here the moment
hasn't passed.

An alien moon
rises. Hearing
birdsong in the forests of the dead
you pin it
in your mind's ear:

my inheritance
redacted
to a prosody; by flow & respiration
stripped to contour,
archipelago.

Even your last wordless sounds
are of that music my mother
grieved in:
I want
to kiss you, to understand,
but I have no body—

The Poet's Mother at Eleven, Killing a Chicken

As for the bird, its pedigree
was impeccable: rose-combed & indigenous

cockfighting in its blood. My grandfather had folded
its ancestor under his arm

in a bolt of jute & the boxcar dark. He was young
& bound for the provinces, fleeing

with his bride the rifled
capital, the Arisaka Type 99, its stock

chrysanthemum-stamped, the blade
jabbed half-jokingly into my grandmother's

stomach: swollen the private thought
not with limbs but a stash.

Dowry; doubloons; maybe
even meat. In the clatter & sway

the hen held its tongue, producing
eggs but no epiphanies

although the flesh of its forebears had delighted
the palates of missionaries, good-

intentioned Baptists in the wake of cholera
& reconcentration: nation builders; tenderfoots;

virgins still wet with honeysuckle & whitewash.
Who brought among other things home

economics, so that fifty years later my mother
would have to corner

& seize it. Wring its wattled links.
Pluck it & gut it & waste

nothing.

Tula

An immigrant's son
I have ears like the blind.

Music comes easily;
night frightens me.

Home late from the hospital, she comes to my door—
I fake sleep.

She sings a soothing song
in the language I never learned:

prayers against rain.
Catalog of mythic birds.

As many names for music
as English has for theft.

Using them I invent
a country with only two citizens.

The word I choose for *mother*
sounds like the one for *dream*.

Notation

Her singing—sight-reading—while we
                 were supposed to be sleeping.

Dad downtown in a tower
                 & thrum of the graveyard shift.

Her piano: even *pianissimo*
                 throbbed the snow-muffled rambler.

Hymns that taught what the word is: a spell
                 for collapsing distances. And folk songs,

her forte, a rep rehearsed for classmates
                 who sometimes passed through:

they'd belt them out together,
                 flower prints crowding the upright.

Afterward cackling in her language:
                 uncrackable, although I thought I caught

the upshot: why here, in this white cold
                 & quiet? As if winter could cure a childhood

of cholera & typhoons. Her hand:
                 she transcribed my favorite melodies

as capitals on scrap paper. I hadn't learned
                 notation, but the keys I could solve, a code

checked against the ear. My brother too
                   & the cousins who came for holidays,

some of them born in Manila:
                   I asked them all to string

songs into letters, caravans
                   braving the whiteout. Everyone played;

some even understood Tagalog.
                   Later not one of us could speak.

Tula

Music comes easily:
on notepads I puzzle out
birds' microtonal scales, the *tala*
in which the song thrush improvises: I untangle
the incomplete anagrams of the 11
Umbric urn rills.

                    My whistles are so accurate the birds
love me: they come to die in the shallow water
of my *e*, and *e*, and *e*.

Tula

One night I am my grandfather.

It's summer; no wind.

My daughter has found
work & love in another world.
The pictures of her son look
almost white.

Her political brother's in prison. The youngest
floats
facedown in a river.

It's a season of abduction.
God is under house arrest.
Doors hang open.

The day before, I saw a man so heavy with blood
his soul couldn't rise out of his body.

I should send word I'm dying but
no one can move, not even
to wipe the sweat from their eyes.

Noon, not a sound: even the songbirds
are under martial law.

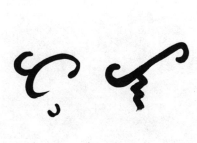

Counting in Tagalog

isa

you say
each sound back to me
gliding up under ash & sycamore

dalawa

a game   echolalia
I'm trying to make up
for lost time

[not time exactly but music]

[not your loss but mine]

tatlo

echolalia a kind of trinity—

a.   echoes like yours; acquisition
b.   ravings of the damaged or ill
c.   a poet's obsession with sound

apat

I started teaching myself last week
& even called my mother

to say so.

        She said two was not *dalawa*
but *duha*.

Ilonggo vs. Tagalog. Not mother tongue
but mother tongues.

lima

        I try
too hard, overpronouncing,
I want to pass so you'll pass
but for whom? When

I was five she brought home a colleague,
a Polish RN with no family, who swore
profusely & well
& loved my mother dearly, especially her singsong
accent.
        But you don't have an accent,
I said. The way she said words
was the best way. The right way, the first.

anim

You're getting drowsy & who wouldn't
the park still thick with night blooms
even though it's almost eleven.

Jasmine: *sampaguita*. Dad says
the scent reminds him of home:
not Minneapolis, but Sampaloc

near the Dangwa Market in Manila.
They sell flowers there but I couldn't find it,
working only from stories he'd told.

pito

A harder pity: sputum
a bystander hawks sideways
warding off bad luck
after crouching to peer in his face—

the struck biker, sprawled. My last day
in Manila. Mad traffic
brought to a standstill; even my lunatic
cabbie held his tongue.

walo

This close to *wala*—none, nothing.
Even extinct.

When we get to ten or eleven
something begins to slow
& harden in the mind

—if the organism does not receive
the appropriate stimulus during this critical period—

siyam

Soon I'll have to stop
or start over,

switch to English, Japanese. Tomorrow
I'll figure out how to turn

1 into 11, 2 into 12, a formula
we'll both unpack as sound.

Nabokov lost sleep
because he couldn't stop counting his heartbeats

& subtracting them from an estimated
total.

       Wild parrots shriek past in a swarm.

I've never seen
how far I could get in this tongue.

sampû

You perk up, almost holler; you love the stressed plosive,
the stoppered air.

I can almost hear you pronounce the diacritic
a roof
pitched against rain

although I've gotten lost & looked
for taxis in it

although it doesn't fall straight & takes
more than cardboard, more

than a sheet of corrugated iron, & my accent
altered the fare.

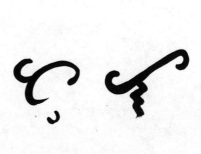

Tula

Like my grandfather
I collect
the songs of birds.

I cut out a music box's heart
& thread a bird's soul into its
star wheel & teeth.

I keep the song of the jay
in plain, unfinished wood;

it has the mark of talent
but a tomboy's voice.

Grackles with their coarse diagnoses
I box up in steel.

The *nejimaki-dori* with the tinker bird
in a clutch of bared clocks.

Mockingbird & icterine warbler
closed in chameleons' skin.

Bombycilla shadei in a Chinese box.

Footnote for the hermit thrush.

Shoebox for the linnet.

Thirteen kinds of blackbirds
in chess-piece cedar—
the queen a black shama.

[Island of the Shy Mynah Bird]

1

Before there were mirrors, there were tide pools.

Before tape recorders, the mynah bird.

2

One *datu* hunts them all into cages:

to protect his people from thinking
they are anything other than island.

You don't have to kill them.

You only have to cut them off
from anything that sounds:

3

soon they cease to be mynahs & become
mere assemblage

matchboxes
swaddled with pappi & moleskin.

4

The second *datu* fills his hall with them
everything he says taken up

& repeated: proclamations, condemnations,
secrets let slip in sleep.

5

They begin to say things he never dared say.

They argue with each other as he would have argued with himself
had he been a more moral man.

Had he had the imagination.

6

He forgets his village.

7

Like a lost colony they fade
into flora & fauna:

rhyme in the albumen.

Oil leached into touched bark.

His dominion a noise of syrinx & back talk,
parallel settings in phase.

8

The third *datu* makes a decree: a mynah for every household.

To pray to: alone, in unison.

To attend carefully as it sings back your sins,
the cage a confessional,
sound booth, shrine.

9

Each moon the birds are brought
to a conference of cages

so that every strain of praise & wrongdoing
can be linked & learned,
mastered.

10

One day, a hut burns to the ground.
Kicked lantern. Dry lightning.

In the confusion, the mynah is set free. It straight-lines
out beyond breakers

cut loose from its loop of encoding & echo:

11

light.   Open ocean.   Island
again.

12

Shy & uncertain
it shifts its weight
above a duff of arrowheads
& irises—

13

is it meat—is it ornament—
a twitch & thrum of archive—

McKinley Praying

Outside the egg of my Allness chuckles the greasy little Eskimo.
Outside the egg of Whitman's Allness too.
    —D. H. LAWRENCE,
        STUDIES IN CLASSIC AMERICAN LITERATURE

Kill every one over ten.
    —GEN. JACOB H. SMITH,
        US SIXTH SEPARATE BRIGADE, 1902

Sometimes like a sultan
I put on a disguise & walk among the people.
The women have Modigliani faces.
The men wear nooses of fire.

I try to tell the soldiers
that every *insurrecto* they grease is Walt Whitman
but they're getting angry & righteous
since he won't lie down or be licked.

I cover him with a blanket
I've just bought from a chuckling Eskimo.
It is many-colored
& uninfected by smallpox.

A murderer lurks among the stalls
but I do nothing to stop him—he's the President
disguised as an actor;
you can tell by his yellow teeth.

One by one he kills my incarnations
while they browse for souvenirs

for my six thousand siblings who have gone
overseas for work.

From his hand he unfurls a bandage
long enough to blindfold
every bronze-skinned boy over the age of ten.
They cock their heads, as if listening.

I hear footsteps behind me.
This is my last life,
a vintage courtesy of a foreign power,
ready to drink & black.

From the window of a nipa hut
Some kind of Indian offers me a wreath—

The Silverest Tongue in the Philippines

after Jaswinder Bolina

I can hear my uncle muttering
in the stillness of his cell.

Bad-mouthing Aguinaldo. Reciting Marx & Mao.

He has the sharpest tongue in the Philippines.

It's why His Excellency the President hates him
& why his doomed brother
worships him.
                                  I can hear him all the way
from Bloomington,
wheedling inside cowrie shells,
in the ice buildup in our gutters.
                                          I won't be born for years
but my ears are preternaturally sharp.

His brother drops out of school
& joins the partisans in Antique.
Picks up where he left off—agrarian
politics & explosives.

Or maybe it's his cellmate
who has the deadliest tongue in the Philippines:

                              but my uncle is alone.
It's the silence I call
his cellmate because he has to give it space,
be wary of its moods.

It's big & oppressive; solitary.

He balls up inside minutes, fissures,
the spoon-dug tunnel of his throat.

                                    Even the shrikes
who are supposed to angle in & give succor
shy away.
He meets me at the terminal
in aviators & a black BMW.
Even I can tell—although I hardly speak

the language—he has the silverest
tongue in the Philippines.

Busboys, shopgirls, investors, bureaucrats, even
the cop he U-turns illegally in front of—
they blush, chuckle, kowtow, make promises

to look out for his nephew
who has the most leaden tongue in the Philippines.

We meet his friends in the lounge of the Shangri-La:
oysters, live music. He doesn't drink
but talks & grows
younger as he does so.
                              Younger even
than I: he has the most golden
tongue in the Philippines. He wins an award—for rhetoric—

& the Palace invites him to fly out & speak. But he gets up,
lashes out
at the President seated behind him:

speaks storm surge, speaks outrage, speaks velocity
& eruption.
                    Now his words are getting muffled:

the blizzards that give birth to me are whiting out his cell.

He's spellbound. Horrified.
Something's finally gotten his tongue. He can hear

a jeep three hundred miles away muttering
up to a checkpoint. Soldiers placing the faces.

His brother makes a break for it
but drops what he's tucked in his shirt; the blast

doesn't kill him
but is followed by a sudden report—

                                        a firearm
making more silence
in a dazed & speechless country.

[Island in the Infinitive]

To survey. To surveil.

To yoke stars, islands,
tribes—slow & far-flung dooms

corralled into ensemble.
To constellate, archipelago.

Portmanteau & neologize.

To fix a golden foil
across the mouth—

burial mask
to keep the evil out.

To raise walled cities,
stone & green with rain.

To reconcentrate (to hamlet).
Keep the evil in.

Upang maging o hindi maging.

To infight. Backstab.
Resort to guerrilla warfare.

To lay it all on questionable wagers.
Submit too readily to fate.

To find no comfort in shade

the Pasig sluggish under the Jones Bridge.

Boys jump down into the weedy slush
brown-limbed, laughing.

To count them, body by body.
Rushing in the ears

like water.

Unfinished Poem

We waste nothing, turn scraps
into feasts of loaves & fishes: shredded,
potpied, spaded into soy-struck rice. You
had to teach me:
                            in shielding me
from her own childhood my mother instilled
a distaste for thrift, the scum
boiled out of bone. For me she wanted
abundance; if there were leftovers
she ate them herself.
                            You learned economy
from your father,
his childhood under occupation, the streets
like nicked & blackened bones. His father
hauled crates of matches
& sugar deep into the country
to trade for potatoes & rice.
                            The crates
their own kind of abundance—a gift, extra
rations from an Oregonian sergeant
who didn't know what *nisei* meant
but recognized the authenticity
of your Ojii-san's Portland accent.

One of those strange recursions of labor,
of downturn & family history: Japanese,
American. Japanese again.
                            Their neighbors carried
pendants, kimonos, teacups—anything
pretty & useless & hard
to find out in the country, whether

there was a war on or not. The rice had to last
for weeks. Still

he managed to scrimp for an LP,
the only one he could get hold of: Schubert's
Symphony no. 8 in B Minor, the Unfinished,
a work no one in his household
particularly liked, but which they listened to
again & again, since it was all that was left
after the world had ended.

[Island of the Little Mouthfuls]

Blown coral.

Fecund stone.

Terraced rain & tricycles.   Rooms

carved out of oilcans, panties, cracker boxes.

Island before breakfast, without its first cigarette.

Island of exported labor.

Fly wings & beauty marks.

Island with a thimbleful of serum. Island

trying to be a better option

for the beached whale.

Comely island

minus its lowermost ribs.

Composite divided by prime.

Island of tautological coastlines.

Skulls flared with jasmine

course-correcting the night sailors.

[Island of Fault Lines]

It was Tōjō.
It was McKinley.
It was Mauser & Krag
& Arisaka & three hundred years
of brands & chalices. It was rain
& the collarbones of women
bloomed by heat & miscegenation.
It was shoes.
It was corrugated iron.
It was homegrown & inequitable.
It was nephews, friends of friends, the good
life that wanted to keep on keeping.
It was smokeless.
It was capital.
It was the logic of the emerging
global market.
It was ramping up.
Bleeding. The prepared-for guest
called away across the water.
It was called across the water
but still it was not American.
It followed this form: *a. wandering*
b. acceptance c. cast out again.
It was hungry. It went to meetings.
It spent a tenth of a day's wages to dance
with Riot & Exclusion.
It was not American.
It learned how to swim
but could still remember not knowing how to swim
& drowned.

It was evening.
It sat at the bottom of the Pacific & listened
to its eyes being eaten.

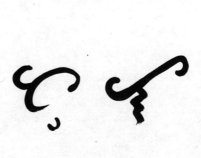

Tula

My friends grow old quick.
They're boxed in the earth
by the time I stop growing. Their hair
keeps growing.

Mother's a sketch in a dream book; memories
of her language get mixed up with melodies
girls I meet hum.

My father leaves the room for a thermometer,
comes back to find me
thirty, with an apartment in Phoenix
& no wife.
                         He shakes his head.
He'll become a hermit now, bits of leaf in his beard.
On the cave wall
the temptations of black angels.

Virginity

It fit too tight, tailored too close,
like something you wear with your hands crossed,
lips sewn shut.
I didn't want to wait, the way I believed
my father had.
                    He was clean like Christ
was supposed to make us—
although I'd steal into his bathroom while
he worked the night shift & rifle *Playboys*
out from under the sink.

                            It was a wonder to find
sex had less to do with me
than I'd thought; she
kicked aside the curtain, saw a red rose,
while I came early & watched her face.

Then I envied my father,
my parents, their garden with no names
or even metaphors for skin,
the river between the trees.

Tula

I don't get any mail
for years, not one bill.

The grass growing past my window
blocks out the sun.

On a winter morning,
in a month that lasts seven years, I receive

a yellowing telegram: from my grandfather.

He wants me to come
because he's dying.

There's postage due, but we're given one coin
in the currency of the dead.

Because I won't give mine up, the bleached postman
eats every word.

Tula

I live mostly in dreams.

From the next cell, a man who says he's my uncle
teaches me our tongue. We work

on colors first, add flora,
fauna, how a man in our bloodline
killed a famous captain.

He has a disease of the lungs;
his breathing worsens.

One day I hear them drag his body out.
I'm alone.

Then a voice rasps from a different cell:
my other uncle, the one whose name
is carved into a wall.

He speaks
the language of the dead, the same one
his brother taught me.
                    The window,
he sings. *The wind.* I cross

oceans, carrying
moisture in my chest feathers.

But I have
no young, no
country to speak of.

My wings grow heavy—
around me, miles
of water & silence.

Photograph: Loggers at Kuala Tahan

To be burned together into wet cells is something not to be taken lightly;

+

only after I swear to send copies do they agree to have it taken.

+

Lank & boot cut, they smoldered against the treeline.

For a living
they laid low the mysteries
for which we'd made our pilgrimage.

+

Kuala they said meant *confluence*.

                                        We drank to it
first emptying our backpackers' bottle
then something sweet & secret
of theirs—

+

                   soon, we understood each other
or thought so:
                dark & large-eyed
quick to befriend or fight.

+

We were kinsmen,
cousins, brothers, split
by lapse & current & soon
to part ways again—for Sarawak.

For home.
For false starts & failed relations. Days
        lashed to this one
only through trade & tariff.

+

And rain—
tail-lit,   unseasonal;   drumming
the cinder blocks of the pharmacy.

                                We've come out
cat-eyed & liquor-bright, crowded
together against a void.

+

The lab tech, a Fijian doubling
as cashier, understands something
of their dubiousness
or else it's the intensity of their wish to have
        in hand
this veranda, this
not being alone, although he loads
only paper
& doesn't bother to make the room

+

dark. Out on the broad lot, even rainwater is refused.

Out on the broad lot, it pools thick as palm oil.

+

                                        Soon they'll fire him
for grinning too sagely or too often
giving comps no one asks for. Soon,

to give notice, I'll hunt
for my landlord's face, somewhere off Wade
fused to its screen door
beside a number I never fail to forget

so that I have to nose among the bougainvillea
& carports, which, besides the river
are all that stays dry:
                        slake & slag
squared to the outrush, forgotten most easily
when crossed.

+

Dingbat & waterway.   Their laughter slashed to the banks.

+

            On the white
of the peeled-off label, one of them
scrawls the address.

Tahan he says means last.

+

                              For them
the forest was what they could see
& because at the end of each day they could
        still see
more than they could cut the next,
they could choose:
                    fire over water.

                                    Stihl over crosshatch.

Smoke over lianas.
                    Dusk over sleep.

+

Below us
the restaurant floats;
the Tahan muddies the Tembeling.

+

                              One of us
had secretly shouldered the Scotch
                from Narita to Jerantut
into shade that had never known ice
                        & consequently teemed with life
so that inside the hide's rain-smattered slats
                we could hold all night
to the idea of tigers.

+

Still I shield the faces

                        so they do not whorl or ruddle
although I've lost what they wrote down

                              & will send the prints
nowhere.

+

We woke to a loop
of birdsong, rising
but never arriving.

+

              Nothing
slung near enough

                    to take stock of us with its stillness
but a troop of backlit macaques

                            too indifferent to change course.

+

Even in the true dark & downpour

                    our breathing
had bent blades.

[Island En Passant]

The piano I built from memory
while stranded on a desert island.

First I had to realize I needed it.
The rest was mostly guesswork.

In the end I had something new
of bark, bamboo & grass—

a ramshackle, a shamble, reeds
in rows like maps of muscle.

It was too heavy to move, so there it stayed
going gray in sun & wind

silent after I was rescued
except for the living things it later housed

afraid of their own infinitesimal steps:
music the stars would make if they

were as small as they looked.

Tula

But there are no undiscovered countries.

When I get to the Land of the Dead
there won't be a mile
of wilderness
of unspoiled earth.

                                        The Kings & Papacy of the Dead
will have sent ships to every continent
to raze temples, to pack slaves,
to scorch the forests & libraries

into cities of black glass.

                                     The aborigines knew

how certain crushed leaves cleanse a murderer's soul;
they knew which mollusks to dive for under the swollen moon,
    whose scraped meat
brings deep sleep, dreams of past lives;
they could catch birds with their hands;
they sewed the feathers into royal garments;
they knew how to find the songbirds' nests & copied their songs to
    make a language;
they copied their language to make songs.
They saw the population spiral down, infinitesimally, until all that
    remained

was a trace, whistling
through the last native speaker on his deathbed
whistling
through his memory's broken teeth.

It will all be slashed, burned.
Smoke over stumped fields.

Like it or not
the Dead keep coming.

Transpacific

She comes by air; she never learned

to swim—seven thousand islands

& not a single stroke. After a certain age

swimming is as impossible

as learning a new language. We call islands

archipelago but the Italians meant the sea.

A better word: *diaspeirein*. Tongues, tribes,

coastlines—scattered

before anyone took flight.

                    From Caticlan

to Kalibo I hardly speak a word.

I keep my mouth shut to pass

although the next passenger might be kin.

My uncle tells me how he kept from going under:

by counting his own breaths.

Jumped into the fishpond

he jumped into as a boy; how he taught himself

to swim. Solitary confinement

is learning how not to drown in time.

No swimming through concrete.

You could swim through blood

but there never seems to be

enough. In one version of his death

my other uncle falls into a river; the bullets

kill him, not the water. Other times

it's the President, his secret police, the First Lady's

tears of sympathy.

                          Lola goes by bus

to gather his remains. Lolo stays behind.

He's anchored, has been all his life

to Jesus & his wheelchair. Can't swim

but he can baptize. He could baptize

a whole town & does. And dies while watching

planes wheel past: a stroke. Gone

but not his gaze, which cuts my flight path

like a searchlight.

                    In indoor swimming pools

you can sometimes hear

your own thirty-year-old laughter; waves

can take that long. My eldest

takes to water easily; I count his strokes

in Japanese—*ichi, ni, san.* He's seven

thousand miles away. Too long

& so I've left him home.

Tulang: poem pluralized to strangeness.

Made nasal, *ng* a sound

that will never start its own word,

not in this tongue. The ghost of an action:

how a gerund blindfolds

a verb to make it still: *come, go.*

Going.

Night Letter to Rilke

Roses, you said, are ruthless in their desire
under so many lids

to be no one's sleep. So you left Ruth
& went walking

barefoot through empty castles
to feel around you the silence

grow wider. But there's always an upbeat.
Always the strung readiness

of knowing that someone might cry out
& who will hear it

if not us. When I saw his new torso
suffused with purple light

as though not our son after all
but an organ—a heart

I'd sung into each night
before they cut him out looking big & angry—

I knew I must change my life. How badly
you wanted to feel your own death

to account cell by cell
for your own body's passing.

Is that so different from enduring the most menial
of tasks, the grind

& counterweight, the tedium & vigilance
of seeming to be a god?

Isn't the preparation to be abandoned
also the prick of the bodied life,

the left arm swelling first,
then the right, finally the body

reduced to a bell?

Hele in C

Hush—hear the wave-lap, the hull-rime
in *lullaby*. English spells for sleep
rudder-cut the North Sea. (Dutch
the hushed root.) Later turns in mother's tongue

to *lalabay*. English spells *force*
by forcing C to cede sibilance. Little imp,
it's late. You root, turn, touch: mother
tongue a boondock song. Do loanwords

imply debt? *Sibile* fore-sings sybil.
Music spells 4/4 C but sounds
lapping waves in three: *lulla, lulla, lullaby*.
Bundok, docked in English, implies a debt

of sound. Forces sheering homeward.
Rudders cut the South Seas, spells
for forcing sleep: the Sulu, the Celebes.
Ply this hushed route; sleep sound.

[Island without Ancestors]

Trade winds glad-hand the dropped husks.
No stroke or syllable has ever been made

to mean bone.
You are first, and alone, and final:

the island an eardrum. The island
a womb through which you catch hints

of the sea & its voices.
Driftwood. Whale song.

Tail end of a squall.
Shoals like a backlit sundress—

soft fire, tombstone, frogspawn,
organ pipe—coral

teeming with damselfish.
The interior a green wall

sheer & Permian.
Karst limestone nested with swiftlets.

ultra / sound

ki-bo[1]   the heart strong & fast

ki-bo   ki-bo[2]   pressed by echo
                                   into light

ki-bo   ki-bo   ki-bo[3]   he stirs when you're
                                   still

                                   bow-grips
                                   for the moth—

ki-bo   ki-bo   ki-bo   ki-bo   ur-music
                                   hope

                                   a homophone
                                   for blood-sound

                                   busong
                                   Ilonggo for

                                   pregnant is pregnant
                                   with song

---

1   Ilonggo/Hiligaynon (noun): the sound the heart makes
2   Tagalog (verb): to move
3   Japanese (noun): hope

Still Life with Transduction

The last time we'd met—a bad quarrelsome
Thanksgiving made worse by partners we

were both about to leave—she'd told me
about the pregnancy, including the Southeast Asian

country from which she believed its soul
had come. It was Oakland, a world away

from the prairie suburb we'd both fled
for love & education, where I'd drawn

mostly from postcards & she'd explained
it was best to draw from life. I said nothing

of comfort—not because I was heartless
but because I was stunned—& she retired

to her prized possession, the claw-foot tub
she'd restored on the second floor

& my last thought before waking in the dark
to drive south over swells & stretches

Midwestern in their shorelessness
was to wonder what it was like to see

with sound: limbs
folded, unfolding, curled in pulse

& process. I took a class to pass the time
in a jobless friendless city: it was important to learn

to feel what I saw, to remember what I touched
touched me. It took years to learn

that with luck you can see the face
& with luck's opposite even stillness.

Soon a postcard came (a favorite Balthus
& a subtext of reconciliation) & in a drizzle

off Fairfax she introduced her husband
& I my wife & infant son. Out of ignorance,

not tact, they made no mention of the one
we hadn't been able to have. She was glowing,

almost three months, & would soon get
her first chance to see. *Tell me*

everything she said, meaning tell me
not to be afraid.

Some Words

It means a new vocabulary:
oxytocin for the bond

that makes mothers shed milk at a wail,
milia for the grainy pimples

on the bridge of his fingernail nose.
And before I've read *lanugo*

the down between his shoulder blades
gone. The scent too: night-

bloom freshness
nape & limb

no name I've found although
if it were an ideogram

I'd write it *rind & aura*
field & fold

cycle that must be tended or
to stoke a little fire

Gloss

as many words for lullaby   as English has for wave—

                                                breaker
                              ripple   roller

                 swell   surge
                                        sound

hili   also envy

lulay   island prayer   [may you still]
                                        [may you strengthen]

                 [may your thrashing turn to heft]

hele   mispronounced as *heal*   /   wakefulness a wound

kantang
· *pampatulog*

                 incantation

                 bearing song's Roman root:

                              [cantata]   [cantabile]

indigenized by *k* but also

                              that much closer to Ithaca

oyayi   altos in Batangas / lull with a *huluna*

huluna   spare in text but rich in fioriture

alaala   waves are part of it

               waves   &   a rhythm

kokli   eardrum   /   a loanword   /
                                           cartilage   & blood-peal

               [no need for it
                         to be re-]
                                   turned

katapusan   archipelago   /   *arkipelago*   /   I scribe

               a seastone in your ear

[Nesology]

. . . the call, from off the shore, of an islandness to come.
—ANTONIS BALASOPOULOS

What matters is a good stroke. Oars cutting the dark. Meanwhile
a word on the tip of your tongue—*scatter, sow, deposit.*

Through the night your mouth has begun to open

wider when you say it, even to yourself, until it tumbles forward
gratefully into wet unremarkable sand,

haphazard shafts of trees. No regularity to their spacing. No key.

The word is tired, for now, of the sea—

it will make do with this sprawl of backbone, these shoots, this
sheltered lagoon.

Its twin, meanwhile, arrives on some other prospect, totaling up the
hues, the curled forms, the riot of coral gusting

that sings more narrowly through it.

Until it shifts. Hardens.

And a new ear is needed, a new music to reconcile their distance,
their dissonance—

Tula

The port where I'll find him is dirty & crowded.

                Talk of war in the newsstands.

Refugees lined up with passports
& bribes
                    for a bureaucratic seal

carved from cowbird skulls—the seal
                        of the Dead.

Bruised & sullen they'll eye me
like a traitor
                        a foreigner
                        a spy

although I'll have come at last
                  to my native land.

Tula

He'll be waiting.

He wants me to go with him
on an expedition: he's one of the ones
who still believe Paradise

will be a kind of library.

+

He has a one-bedroom flat. A window on the gray sea.
Keepsakes & projects to while away the hours:

    an ancient cracked urn with a frieze of musicians, birds & danc-
    ers;

    sketches for an alphabet with three versions of the vowel *e*;

    drafts for patterns of kinship; passport photos for a boy;

    our race's lost music, reconstructed

        from little evidence
                                       (images
      on an urn
                                         light
    trapped in skulls
                            cognates in birdsong)

                  the way you can determine

    the Etruscan word for Etruscan.

Tula

Down on the street I see
we're the same age

he's getting
younger

I had something
I wanted to tell him

but I'm already forgetting
my name

Tula

Little waif—mudlark—why
do I follow you

down to the shore's gray light?
I can't keep up

& the sea is cold
you call out a name that must be

mine
but the outriggers

already glide to the deep
there you are   clinging

to the gunwale
weeping strange

elderly tears
into the low creak of oars

off in mist your slender craft
dissolves

I wave & try to smile
but my heart
slumps

as if we were blood & not
strangers.

Tula

Goodbye, little stranger.

If you should find yourself
shipwrecked
shivering in starlit solitude

open your hand
bitten deep
by my parting gift—open

my gift.   Broken
you'll think
radiating nothing into space

save silence.

                        But on the edge of it
delicate as the fearful
breath of lovers in a next room

                                     something rises:
like a light echo thinning
but not dying:

causing something far off & crystalline
to tremble into music—

A Year in the Snow Country

                              Later I married, in
the careless zoning of the American West,
the sense of not only all the time in the world but
the space too.
                         Amid the sun-struck strip malls
of Torrance & Gardena we found markets
that smelled like Tohoku's:
stalls with stewing pork-bone broth;
skate & mackerel bright
with brine & ice; flags
of *komachi* rice bento'd
& bloodshot with *umeboshi*: & daikon
cut down to spindles—

                              radishes I'd seen
grow long as oars
washed white of earth & draped
to dry from the eaves of farmhouses;
roofs thatched of water reed
winter-cut & singed to strong
stems, steep-sloped against one hundred
and eighty days of powder & drizzle; all that rain
& reckless growth—

                         grated, to help my mother-in-law,
a fierce & endless task
to produce a mere garnish, mild as apple,
pinched raw with cheek
of blackened pike; this side of
root & *accumulation*.

Where the Fathers Wait

He hadn't turned & they were going to rip him out
& he started to come anyway
so they ripped him out in the dead of night.

They took him somewhere

& somewhere below the sheet
your body was still open: we aren't meant
to see the mess inside us, to see

ourselves turned inside out: we need

the priest to go behind the curtain
because even in passing, the sight of God
will finish us for good.

Later the newborn smell will fade

into something less clean & more human;
later the rooting & hardcover heft. Closed
up again your skin

falls like bread & it could have had more

to do with *us*, I think,
instead of being a process we witnessed.
But the pain catches up

& the scar recedes obscenely

as if it were all coming undone; as if
no price had to be paid, which is what *presence*
really means: a remote outpost, perhaps

night, perhaps in another world, where

a door opens & your name
is called & all at once you aren't cut off anymore
from the rest of the world: you are

the rest of the world.

Hele

little monsoon
little fist
& groundswell

they lay you out in naked light
tagged like an ashy thrush

little stroke   blood-peal
riptide
displaced by a scissor kick

there are no more oceans to cross
just the same we'll let you go

but not today
today

you are a room
words crisp as fresh-cut eyelets

today you are a bell
pitched just high of mine

so that when I sound we sway
like boats

no blood conduction   no diastole

still you recognize the shoreline
unshrouded
beaten bronze

what we sang to you each night

you fold it in your hand
it cools   keeps

even far out of earshot
deep
in a chirring shoreless continent

Notes

Note on Filipino characters: the Filipino alphabet known as *baybayin* is an abugida, or segmental writing system, that predates the Spanish colonization of the Philippines. In *baybayin*, ᜆᜓ is the character for TU, and ᜎ is the character for LA. *Baybay* means "to spell."

"[Island of the Shy Mynah Bird]": There are nearly 400 million speakers of Austronesian languages, which include Malay, Javanese, and Tagalog. The "[Island]" poems and "Photograph: Loggers at Kuala Tahan" imagine the heritage of Austronesian navigation and migration shared by this diaspora, which includes peoples and cultures of Asia and the Pacific.

"The Poet's Mother at Eleven, Killing a Chicken": The Type 99 Arisaka is a bolt-action rifle, used by the Japanese Imperial Army during World War II. Reconcentration was employed by the US military during the Philippine-American War (1898–1902/13). The practice involved uprooting civilians and relocating them to camps; it resulted in starvation and outbreaks of cholera and dysentery. As many as one million Filipinos died during the war and subsequent occupation.

"Counting in Tagalog": In linguistics, the "critical period" describes the stage at which language is most readily acquired; it is thought to end sometime between five years of age and puberty. The various meanings of *echolalia*, including the repetition of speech sounds by language-learning children, are drawn from Julia Kristeva. Ilonggo is a common name for Hiligaynon, an Austronesian language spoken in the Visayan region of the Philippines.

"Tula" ("Like my grandfather"): *Nejimaki-dori*, or "wind-up bird," is an invention of Haruki Murakami. A star wheel is a disk that functions as a ratchet in repeating watches, music boxes, and other machines. The black shama or *Copsychus cebuensis* is a songbird endemic to the Visayan region of the Philippines, and is listed by the IUCN Red List as Endangered.

"Virginity" paraphrases a tanka by Yosano Akiko (1878–1942) (trans. Atsumi Ikuko): "Holding my breasts / I softly kicked the mysterious door open; / The crimson flower here is deep."

"[Island in the Infinitive]" contains a Tagalog translation of the opening line of Hamlet's soliloquy in Act III. During the American War in Vietnam, reconcentration (see note above) was referred to as "hamletting."

"[Island of Fault Lines]" paraphrases a passage from Franz Kafka's diaries.

"McKinley Praying": William McKinley, president of the United States, in the *Christian Advocate*: "I walked the floor of the White House . . . and I am not ashamed to tell you . . . that I went down on my knees and prayed Almighty God for light and guidance. . . . And one night late it came to me . . . that there was nothing left for us to do but to take them all. . . . The next morning I sent for the chief engineer of the War Department . . . and I told him to put the Philippines on the map of the United States."

Following an insurgent victory known as the Balangiga Massacre, Gen. Jacob H. Smith of the Sixth Brigade ordered his men to kill every male Filipino child over the age of ten. A political cartoon published by the *New York Journal* on May 5, 1902, shows several blindfolded Filipino boys standing in front of a firing squad. Leon Czolgosz, who assassinated McKinley in 1901 at the Pan-American Exposition in Buffalo, New York, kept his gun hand wrapped in a bandage or handkerchief.

"The Silverest Tongue in the Philippines" is for Fluellen Ortigas (b. 1948, Jaro, Philippines) and for Virgil Ortigas (b. 1952, Jaro, Philippines; d. 1973, Antique, Philippines). It takes its form from Jaswinder Bolina's poem "The Tallest Building in America."

"Unfinished Poem" is for Kazuta Takasugi (b. 1919, Portland, Oregon; d. 2010, Monterey Park, California).

"Photograph: Loggers at Kuala Tahan": Kuala Tahan is a village and staging post for travelers entering Malaysia's Taman Negara (National Park), a 130 million-year-old rainforest. Since Taman Negara is one of the world's oldest rainforests and never experienced glaciers or an ice age, its biodiversity is unique and stunning. It is also under threat due to the region's rapidly increasing rates of deforestation.

"Transpacific": *Diaspeirein*, the Greek source of *diaspora*, carries the additional connotations of "scatter, sow, deposit." This poem, and several others in the collection, refer to Fluellen Ortigas's imprisonment as a dissident by the Marcos administration, much of it in solitary confinement, and the shooting of Virgil Ortigas by the administration's secret police.

"Night Letter to Rilke" is dedicated to Oliver de la Paz, Srikanth Reddy, and Li-Young Lee, for their invaluable insights into being both parents and poets. It adapts lines from "Archaic Torso of Apollo" (trans. Stephen Mitchell), and from the first of the *Duino Elegies* (trans. David Young). The end of the poem refers to a myth about Rilke's death, as retold by William Gass.

"Hele in C": The phrase "debt of sound" is borrowed from Brandon Som's poem "Elegy."

"Gloss": Each entry is a synonym for *lullaby*, except for the last three: *alaala* (memory), *kokli* (cochlea), and *katapusan* (denouement). *Huluna* is a specialized lullaby form from the province of Batangas, characterized by elaborate vocal embellishments (fioritura) on simple texts.

"[Nesology]": The epigraph comes from Antonis Balasopoulos's article "Nesologies: Island Form and Postcolonial Geopoetics."

"Tula" ("Little waif"): "strange / elderly tears" is adapted from a line by Franz Wright.

"A Year in the Snow Country": Akita, a rural prefecture in northern Japan, is famous for its *komachi* rice, whose flavor is supposedly enhanced by the region's ample rain and snow.

In Japanese, *daikon* is written as 大根, with the second ideogram meaning "root." The character 積, or *seki*, can be used to describe the accumulation or "piling up" of snow (or grated vegetables), but can also be used to write *tsumori*, or "intention."

"Hele": The *Zoothera cinerea* or ashy thrush is endemic to the Philippines and is listed by the IUCN Red List as Vulnerable.

Acknowledgments

Thank you to the following publications, where these poems first appeared, sometimes in different forms:

Adroit Journal: "Night Letter to Rilke"
Anamesa: "[Island En Passant]"
Asian American Literary Review: "Tula" (as "Tula for Voice, Music Box, and Extinct Birds")
Copper Nickel: "tu la," "Hele"
Dusie: "Gloss"
FIELD: "A Year in the Snow Country," "Hele in C," "Unfinished Poem"
Ghost Town: "Notation," "Transpacific," "[Island of the Little Mouthfuls]"
Kartika Review: "Audiometry," "Where the Fathers Wait"
Lantern Review: "Some Words"
The Offending Adam: "The Silverest Tongue in the Philippines," "[Island without Ancestors]"
Postcolonial Text: "McKinley Praying," "The Poet's Mother at Eleven, Killing a Chicken," "Photograph: Loggers at Kuala Tahan," "[Island of Fault Lines]" (as "Fault Lines")
Revolver: "Virginity"
TAYO Literary Magazine: "[Island of the Shy Mynah Bird]," "[Nesology]"

"[Island of Fault Lines]" also appeared in the anthology *VERSES TYPHOON YOLANDA: A Storm of Filipino Poets*, ed. Eileen Tabios (San Francisco & Saint Helena: Meritage Press, 2014).

I would like to extend my deepest thanks to A. Van Jordan, Daniel Slager, Patrick Thomas, Joey McGarvey, Mary Austin Speaker, Patricia Kirkpatrick, and all of the wonderful people at Milkweed Editions and the Lindquist & Vennum Foundation.

For their generous attention, advice, and encouragement while I was developing this manuscript, I am grateful to David St. John, Susan McCabe, Brandon Som, Joshua Rivkin, Joy Katz, Oliver de la Paz, Cathy Linh Che, Mark Irwin, Scott Reding, Marjorie Perloff, Carol Muske-Dukes, Fox Henry-Frazier, and Stewart Grace.

For their wisdom, insight, and support, I am grateful to Janalynn Bliss, Viet Nguyen, Bruce Smith, Wayne Miller, Pamela Alexander, Martha Collins, David Young, Stuart Friebert, Li-Young Lee, Srikanth Reddy, Gerald Maa, Eugenia Leigh,

Iris Law, Mia Malhotra, Luke Finsaas, Chad Sweeney, Cody Todd, Andrew Wessels, Tarfia Faizullah, David Walker, Diane Vreuls, Eileen Tabios, Martha Collins, Margaret Rhee, Neil Aitken, Jennifer Feeley, Danielle Peterson Searls, Damion Searls, Sean Finney, Sarah Gambito, Joseph Legaspi, and Kundiman.

Thank you to Fluellen Ortigas, kin and guide; thank you to the good people of Bantayog ng Bayani, for preserving the memory of Virgil and Gaston Ortigas and the many others who courageously resisted martial law.

My most heartfelt thanks to Rene Santiago, Dr. Tsuneo and Tomoko Takasugi, Tommy and Lisa Vuong, Dr. Eric Takasugi and Alex Takasugi, and Sean and Connie Santiago. Thank you too to Aki and Tristan, for your patience and intuition and joy. Thank you most of all to Yuri: this book is for you.

And finally, to my mother, Mildred Ortigas Santiago (1946–2015): thank you for the gift of language; I will keep listening closely for your voice.

JOANNA DEMKIEWICZ

CHRIS SANTIAGO is the author of poems, fiction, and criticism that have appeared in *FIELD*, *Copper Nickel*, *Pleiades*, and the *Asian American Literary Review*. He holds degrees in creative writing and music from Oberlin College and received his PhD in English from the University of Southern California. The recipient of fellowships from Kundiman and the Mellon Foundation/American Council of Learned Societies, Santiago is also a percussionist and amateur jazz pianist. He teaches literature, sound culture, and creative writing at the University of St. Thomas. He lives in Minnesota.

The fifth award of

THE LINDQUIST & VENNUM PRIZE FOR POETRY

is presented to

CHRIS SANTIAGO

by

MILKWEED EDITIONS
and
THE LINDQUIST & VENNUM FOUNDATION

Established in 2011, the annual Lindquist & Vennum Prize for Poetry awards $10,000 and publication by Milkweed Editions to a poet residing in North Dakota, South Dakota, Minnesota, Iowa, or Wisconsin. Finalists are selected from among all entrants by the editors of Milkweed Editions. The winning collection is selected annually by an independent judge. The 2016 Lindquist & Vennum Prize for Poetry was judged by A. Van Jordan.

Milkweed Editions is one of the nation's leading independent publishers, with a mission to identify, nurture, and publish transformative literature, and build an engaged community around it. The Lindquist & Vennum Foundation was established by the Minneapolis-headquartered law firm of Lindquist & Vennum, LLP, and is a donor-advised fund of The Minneapolis Foundation.

Walbaum is a German Modern typeface created in the Didone style invented by Justus Erich Walbaum (1768–1839), a type designer who trained as a spice merchant, pastry chef, and coin cutter. Inspired by the work of Firmin Didot in France and Giambattista Bodoni in Italy, Walbaum's design uses sharper contrast between thick and thin strokes and a squareness to the characters. Justus Walbaum's designs have been listed as an influence on nineteenth-century sans serif typefaces such as Univers and Helvetica.

Interior designed and typeset by Mary Austin Speaker